# *The* Cook Book

Published by
On The Eighth Day Co-operative Ltd
111 Oxford Road
Manchester
M1 7DU


Photography Jon Moss and Sean Bish
Illustration Alex Hargreaves
Recipes and text researched and written by Café workers past and present


© On The Eighth Day Co-operative Ltd 1999


British Library Cataloguing-in Publication Data.
A catalogue record for this book is available from the British Library

ISBN 0 9536549 0 7

# contents

| | |
|---|---|
| *Introduction* | **1** |
| *A brief history of On The Eighth Day Co-operative Ltd* | **3** |
| *General Notes* | **5** |
| *Oven Temperature Chart* | **7** |
| *Measurement Chart* | **8** |
| *Soups* | **9** |
| *Stews* | **18** |
| *Salads* | **32** |
| *Bakes* | **42** |
| *Puddings* | **70** |
| *Index* | **79** |

# introduction

For as long as anyone can remember, the one constant question that customers in the Café have asked is, "When are you going to write a recipe book?" Well here it is, we hope it was worth waiting for!

The recipes in this collection are the favourite dishes produced by the Café. Some are so old, their origins are lost in the mists of time whilst others are fairly recent additions to the menu.

For a long time now, we have run the Café with seven members who work full time, and all cook on a rota basis, usually a couple of times a week. We now use standard recipes and fortnightly menus. In the good old days, we just left it up to the individual to decide what to cook. This did lead to some interesting experimental work, not always appreciated by the long suffering customer.

Obviously, the recipes as used in the Café make enormous quantities. Our stew pan, for example, holds six gallons. To produce a version that will make 4 portions, has been a truly co-operative venture, with all the Café workers 'test driving' a selection until it worked. Sometimes this has meant changing recipes slightly, as cooking in bulk does not always translate easily into smaller amounts.

The end results are as close as you can get to Eighth Day food at home, which should please all you regular Café customers. If you have never eaten in our Café, buy the book anyway, it is all good vegetarian whole food and has all the cooking experience of every Café worker since 1971 built in - what a bonus!

We have designed the recipes so that they can be made by the complete novice cook - so apologies to any master chefs among you. Obviously the more experienced cook will be able to use these recipes as a basis for further variations on the theme of vegetarian cookery.

If you have any problems or queries please ask us, but avoid lunch times, as you may get your head bitten off by a stressed-out worker!

We intend this to be the first of a series. The next will feature recipes from our Gourmet Evening menus. With a bit of luck it will not take 15 years to produce, but don't hold your breath, just in case!

# A brief history of On The Eighth Day Co-operative Ltd

As the Sixties rushed to a psychedelic end in the blaze of love and chemicals that heralded the dawn of a New Age, a right-on group of friends had their stab at creating a new order. They wanted to establish a way of trading goods that broke away from the ideas of money and commerce. To that end they founded 'On The Eighth Day' as a craft exchange and alternative centre, situated above a boutique in New Brown Street - long since vanished under the Arndale Centre in Manchester.

On the seventh day God rested, on the eighth day He (She or It) created something better. That was the idea of the moment in 1970, when trading commenced. It was a great place to tune in and drop out, but as an attempt to escape the clutches of capitalism it was less successful, and soon had to become a shop in the more conventional sense, in order to survive.

The involvement with the community did not die however. The number of drug addicts in the area was a constant worry, and the charity Lifeline was founded as a result of a collaboration with On The Eighth Day, the Bishop of Middleton and Dr. Eugenie Cheesmond, an expert in the treatment and rehabilitation of addicts.

Meanwhile the business was going through a tough time and when the boutique burnt down, it brought things to a halt. This crisis seemed to redirect the energies of the partners, the insurance money certainly did. In 1972 they reopened here at 111 Oxford Road. We have since discovered the cause of the fire to be faulty wiring installed by an apprentice electrician, but he is paying us too much for his name ever to be revealed.

Once established here, we stayed. Changing from a clothes shop to a whole food shop with clothes. As the interests of the workers in a vegetarian, whole food diet grew, a corner of the shop became a vegetarian café. In the early 1980s the Co-operative managed to buy the whole block and the Café moved next door into 109, and in 1994 into 107 as well.

Since we first settled here the business has had to evolve to keep up with the changing times. The Shop gave up clothes very early on and concentrated on vegetarian whole food. This is still the main staple, now mostly organic if possible, and including many specialist items - Japanese vegetarian food for example. In response to customer's requests we now sell a large range of complimentary remedies, supplements, cosmetics and fair-traded gifts.

For the first six years the business was run as a co-operative but was in fact legally a partnership. In 1976 On The Eighth Day Co-operative Limited registered as a workers' co-operative under the provident societies act. This means that all the full-time workers in the business, currently 10, become members of the Co-operative and both work and manage the business. These days we have to be businesslike to survive but have not lost our ethics. The food is still vegetarian and we try to be as 'green' as possible. We are still involved in striving towards a better world, hopefully one that pays a decent wage!

# general notes

This is the usual boring chapter that it seems has to be included in every cookery book, so why should we fly in the face of convention?

First of all words about nutrition and all that stuff. We do not want to go on much about diet and health, if you need more information there are plenty of books on nutrition around. A sensible diet will be your first line of defence against ill health. Of course the problem can be what you interpret as sensible, most vegetarian experts agree that for good health you need to eat as much unprocessed food as you can. Brown rice, wholemeal bread, plenty of fruit and vegetables, for example, to give a relatively high fibre diet. Even the current advice from the Government, to eat five portions of fruit and vegetables a day, echoes what vegetarian 'cranks' have been saying since the last century!

The more raw fruit and vegetables you eat the better, especially if they are grown organically. In fact you should be careful about pesticide residues in conventionally produced vegetables. That is why our recipes keep on stressing the need to peel them. Little wonder that an interest in healthy eating often leads to a healthy interest in vegetable gardening! Sugar and salt should be avoided or reduced and fats, especially the saturated fats, kept to a minimum. Fat cannot be missed out entirely, the body does not function properly without the essential fatty acids, but the fats found in processed foods and heat treated cooking oils should be avoided. Use cold pressed oils, especially olive, flax seed and sunflower where possible.

The great thing about your food is that it should be interesting and tasty. All too often, when people decide to give up meat, they literally do just that. They are then left with the two veg. part of the traditional, British diet, which is a bit boring to say the least. The last thirty years has seen the development of an International Vegetarian cuisine. This has resulted in British vegetarians adopting and adapting recipes from all over the world which have no need for meat to make them nutritious and tempting.

Some of our recipes may have the same name as a traditional dish but there the similarity ends. All of them are tasty and not one of them is boring.

In the introduction, we said that the recipes were laid out in such a way as to be easy to use for the absolute beginner. It may be useful to have a general talk about kitchen equipment and techniques. There has been a long running debate about the metals suitable for pans - aluminium has been implicated in some research into the causes of degenerative brain disease and so it is probably best to avoid aluminium pans if possible. Both stainless steel and enamel have had adverse publicity at times, but not to the same extent. The only metal to be free from all adverse comment to date, is plain cast iron. In fact, cooking in cast iron gives you iron in your diet! Obviously you will be ruled in part by what you can afford but, certainly from the point of view of performance, cast iron is hard to beat - either plain or enamelled. Next best is good quality stainless steel - the sort with a heavy, laminated base to spread the heat.

The next most important thing in the kitchen is a sharp knife. What you buy will be governed by cost and what you are used to, unless you are not used to using anything. Here at Eighth Day we have used all manner of knives including Chinese vegetable cleavers, Japanese cleavers (which are like razors and still preferred by some cooks) and the whole range of traditional European-style cooks knives. Whatever you use, keep it sharp. A blunt knife is useless and more dangerous than a sharp one, as it slips more easily but is still sharp enough to cut you and not the carrot.

Most people collect an assortment of kitchen gadgets over time. Some are useful like wooden spoons and colanders, others seem a good idea but gather dust in the back of a draw until they get thrown away. One really useful thing is a good balloon whisk. It is better than most other sorts of whisking implement for beating eggs and general mixing. The only electrical gadget we would consider essential, is a blender of some sort. The new stick blenders are very good and reasonably priced. We use a domestic model in the kitchen, for small batches of sauce, and a huge professional stick blender which will can blend a whole five gallon pan of soup in one go. Goblet blenders work all right, but are not quite as convenient to use. If you have not got or cannot afford a blender, do not despair, our ancestors managed to produce smooth pastes without electricity. If everything is well cooked, you can rub the solids through a sieve with a wooden spoon in the traditional way. This is messy and time consuming and you will lose all the fibrous bits. This makes the alternative of learning to love lumpy soups quite appealing.

Another great cookery book tradition is conversion tables, here are some for you to ignore:

# oven temperature chart

These temperatures are for a conventional oven. If you have a fan oven you will need to cook at a cooler temperature - usually about 10°C less - but check in your oven hand book. For combi-microwaves and such - you will just have to make it up as you go along.

| Temperature | Celsius°C | Fahrenheit°F | Gas mark |
|---|---|---|---|
| Very cool | 110 | 225 | ¼ |
| Cool | 120 | 250 | ½ |
| Warm | 140 | 275 | 1 |
| Moderate | 150 | 300 | 2 |
| Fairly hot | 170 | 325 | 3 |
| Hot | 180 | 350 | 4 |
| Very hot | 190 | 375 | 5 |
| | 200 | 400 | 6 |
| | 220 | 425 | 7 |
| | 230 | 450 | 8 |
| | 250 | 500 | 9 |

# measurement chart

We think we have given all the metric equivalents to imperial measures in the recipes, but just in case you need it, here is a table roughly rounded to the nearest 5 grammes or millilitres. Use one set of measurements or the other to save confusion. If you do not possess a set of scales don't worry too much, there are those among us who do not measure anything and it usually works. As a rough guide a rounded tablespoon of flour is about 1 ounce.

| Ounces (oz) | Grammes (g) | Fluid ounces (floz) | Millilitres (ml) |
|---|---|---|---|
| $\frac{1}{2}$ | 15 | 1 | 25 |
| 1 | 25 | 2 | 50 |
| $1\frac{1}{2}$ | 40 | 3 | 75 |
| 2 | 50 | 4 | 125 |
| 3 | 75 | 5 ($\frac{1}{4}$ pint) | 150 |
| 4 ($\frac{1}{4}$ lb) | 100 | 6 | 175 |
| 5 | 150 | 7 | 200 |
| 6 | 175 | 8 | 225 |
| 7 | 200 | 9 | 250 |
| 8 ($\frac{1}{2}$ lb) | 225 | 10 ($\frac{1}{2}$ pint) | 300 |
| 9 | 250 | 11 | 325 |
| 10 | 300 | 12 | 350 |
| 11 | 325 | 15 ($\frac{3}{4}$ pint) | 450 |
| 12 ($\frac{3}{4}$ lb) | 350 | 17 | 500 |
| 13 | 375 | 20 (1 pint) | 600 |
| 14 | 400 | 21 | 625 |
| 16 (1 lb) | 450 | | |

As you use or play about with the recipes, you will find what works for you and what tastes you prefer. Alter anything you like, experiment, go crazy but tell us if you create something marvellous - so we can pinch it for the menu! Of course the down side is that if you have any problems or criticisms, we will do our best to help if you contact us at:

On The Eighth Day Co-operative Limited, 111 Oxford Road, Manchester, M1 7DU.
Phone and Fax: 0161 273 4878
e-mail: 8th-day@eighthy.demon.co.uk
WWW: http://www.eighthy.demon.co.uk

# soups

The word 'soup' can conjure up so many images. From the lightest consommé, to great pans of thick country vegetables which are a meal in themselves and cross into the territory of 'stew'. Here at Eighth Day, our soups served in the Café are always vegan. They tend to be on the hearty side, as along with a roll or two, it will be the main meal of the day for many customers. We usually thicken our soups with potato or pulses and not flour. It helps those people avoiding wheat and is easier for the cook. Most of the soups are simple to make and are a good introduction to cookery for children keen to get among the pots and pans.

# carrot & coriander soup

*The first soup in this collection is elegantly simple. A good winter warmer, it is also delicious as a light lunch. The flavours of carrot and coriander complement each other very well, especially if you are lucky enough to have just pulled the carrots from your own garden. Serves 4.*

- 1 lb (450g) carrots
- 1 medium sized potato
- 1 small onion
- small bunch of fresh coriander
- 1 dessertspoon sunflower oil
- salt and pepper
- 2 ¾ pints (1.5 litres) water

Put the water into a saucepan that will hold at least four pints (3 litres) of liquid, and bring to the boil.

Whilst the water is heating, scrub the potato and carrots (peel if not organic) and chop finely. Put the potato and carrots carefully into the pan. When the water comes back to the boil, turn down the heat and leave to simmer with the lid on.

Peel and chop the onion and, in a separate pan on a moderate heat, fry in the sunflower oil. When the onion is soft and golden, add to the contents of the saucepan. Try not to burn the onion as it will not improve the taste.

Leave the soup cooking and wash the coriander, then chop it very finely.

Test the vegetables in the soup. The carrot and potato need to be quite soft, in fact the softer the better as it makes the next bit easier.

The next bit. Blend the soup. If you have no means of blending, just mash up the vegetables as much as you can.

Finally, add the chopped coriander, stir and season to taste.

# split pea & mint soup

*When we first started making this recipe, back in the early 1980's, we called it "Persian pea soup", (strangely enough because it was from the near east and contained peas). We changed the name because of continual mocking cries of "What have split peas to do with Persia?" Shortly afterwards a customer exclaimed in rapture "This is wonderful, this is soup like we eat in Iran!" We rest our case, but could not be bothered to change the name back. It's a good soup whether it's from Persia or Preston. Serves 4.*

8 oz (225g) green split peas
2 pints (1.2 litres) water
1 medium onion
1 dessertspoon sunflower oil
1 teaspoon shoyu
1 heaped dessertspoon dried mint
salt and pepper

Rinse the peas several times in cold water and drain.

Put the water in a large saucepan, add the peas and bring to the boil, stirring occasionally to prevent the peas sticking. Once boiling turn down the heat, partially cover the pan and simmer gently.

Whilst the peas are cooking, peel and chop the onion finely.

Heat the sunflower oil in a pan over a medium heat, add the chopped onion and gently fry until soft, adding the shoyu once the onions start to cook.

When the onions are soft and have absorbed the shoyu, add them to the boiling peas. Stir in the mint and bring back to the boil.

Cover the pan and simmer until the peas are soft, which will take about an hour. Stir the soup from time to time. If it seems to be getting too thick, add a little water. This soup tends to stick and burn once the peas begin to fall so be warned, keep the light low and stir frequently.

Once the peas have collapsed (but hopefully not the cook) season to taste and serve.

# broccoli soup

*This is another of our most enduringly popular recipes. Both variations are good, old English winter warmers and about the easiest things you could cook, apart from boiling an egg. If you are vegan, forget the egg. Serves 4.*

1 medium onion
1 lb (450g) broccoli
1 large potato, about 12oz (350g)
1 dessertspoon sunflower oil
1 dash of shoyu
salt and pepper

Peel and chop the onion finely. Put the oil in a large saucepan on a medium heat. Add the onions and fry gently until tender, turning the heat down if necessary.

Wash the broccoli and the potato, peeling the potato if it is not organic, and cut them into fairly small pieces, using the stem of the broccoli as well as the florets.

When the onions are soft, add the water, shoyu, potato and broccoli. Bring to the boil and simmer until tender.

Once the potato is cooked blend and season with salt and pepper.

If you want you can use cauliflower instead of broccoli, two for the price of one!

# lentil & coconut soup

*If you are looking for something really smooth, creamy and satisfying that is not served in a pint glass, then look no further. Creamed coconut and lentils just seem to go together like all the best similes! Serves 4.*

- 2 ½ pints (1.5 litres) water
- 1 block creamed coconut
- 8 oz (225g) red lentils
- 1 medium onion
- 1 tin (14oz, 400g) peeled plum tomatoes, or chopped tomatoes
- bunch parsley
- 1 dessertspoon sunflower oil
- salt and pepper

Peel and chop the onions finely and fry in a large pan with the oil until soft.

Meanwhile wash the lentils in several changes of water.

When the onions are soft add the water to the onion pan. Add the lentils and bring to the boil, stirring occasionally to prevent them from sticking.

Add the coconut. It is better if you can break it or cut it into pieces first. Turn down the heat and simmer, stir every now and then, and remove any foam.

Strain the liquid from a tin of tomatoes into the pan and then chop or blend the tomatoes before adding them as well. If you've splashed out on a tin of chopped tomatoes, just pour them in. Bring back to the simmer and cover.

Keep an eye on the soup as it simmers and make sure that, as the lentils cook, they do not absorb all the liquid and begin to burn. If it threatens to become solid rather than liquid, add more water! Cook until the lentils become a smooth paste - this can take up to an hour.

Wash and finely chop the parsley, add to the pan, season and serve.

# tomato & basil soup

*Cook the following recipe and feel the hot Tuscan sun beating down as you smell the olive oil and basil blending into the tomato and garlic. Pass me the Chianti this minute, I can feel an aria coming on! Serves 4.*

2 ½ pints (1.5 litres) water
1 tin (14oz, 400g) peeled plum tomatoes
2 tablespoons tomato purée
1 onion
1 large potato
3 to 4 cloves garlic
2 tablespoons olive oil
2 teaspoons dried basil or a small handfull of fresh basil, if you have it
salt and pepper

Peel and chop the onion. Peel and crush or chop the garlic (There is no need to crush the garlic unless you are dying to use your new garlic press).

Heat the olive oil in a large saucepan. Add the onion and garlic and fry gently until soft.

Meanwhile wash and chop the potato, peeling if not organic.

When the onion is golden brown, add the water to the pan. Put in the potato and bring to the boil.

Once boiling, add the tomatoes, together with the tomato purée. Stir well, cover and simmer gently.

Fresh basil should be washed and roughly chopped then added to the soup, saving a few leaves for garnish. Dried basil can just be tossed in with a suitable Latin flourish.

Cook until the potatoes are soft, then blend and season to taste.

It tastes even better if you garnish it with a few, pitted, black olives and those fresh basil leaves you saved.

# mulligatawny

*The recipe below has a complicated history. It was originally pinched, for want of a better culinary verb, from a very old Eliza Acton original, dating from the early nineteenth century. The Café multiplied it up into our usual vast quantities and it has been a favourite for the last dozen years. Each new cook has altered it slightly, as is the way of things here. Now of course, we've reduced it back down to a domestic quantity for this book. We could have just used the original but no one can remember what it was. In any event it is a fine example of that most British institution, a thoroughly anglicised Indian dish. Serves 4.*

- 4 oz (125g) red lentils
- 1 small potato
- 8 oz (225g) carrots
- 1 small turnip or swede, (about 4oz, 100g)
- 1 parsnip
- 1 courgette
- 1 onion
- 1 tin (14oz, 400g) chopped tomatoes
- 1 tablespoon tomato purée
- 1 teaspoon garam masala
- 1 teaspoon curry powder
- 1 dessert apple
- 2 pints (1.2 litres) water
- 2 dessert spoons sunflower oil
- salt and pepper

Peel and dice the onion. Heat the oil in a saucepan and add the onion. Fry gently with the garam masala and curry powder.

Whilst the onion is frying, wash the lentils under cold running water. It is easier to put them in a sieve. As soon as the onion is soft, add the water to the pan and put in the lentils. Turn up the heat.

Wash the vegetables, peeling any that are not organic. Dice into ½ to 1 inch chunks and add to the pan, along with the chopped tomatoes and the purée.

Once the soup begins to boil, stir, then lower the heat and allow to simmer.

Wash, core and small dice the apple and add to the pan.

Cover and simmer for approximately 1 hour, until all the vegetables are cooked.

Season to taste and serve. This soup is a complete meal for four or could be a starter for 6.

# french onion soup

*The last soup in the collection is another favourite but not so old. This particular recipe has only been made in the Café for 6 or 7 years. Our tribute to French cuisine, or as has been remarked, a soup that shows how much the English really despise the French! Serves 4.*

2 large onions
2 tablespoons white flour
2 tablespoons vegetable oil
1 tablespoon soya sauce
1 teaspoon Hungarian paprika
2 teaspoons English mustard powder
1 large sprig parsley
1 French onion stock cube
2 pints (1.2 litres) water
1 teaspoon molasses

Peel and cut the onions in half and then slice thinly.

Put the vegetable oil in the saucepan on a moderate heat and sauté the onions. Once they start to cook, add the soya sauce and carry on cooking until soft.

Add the flour and allow to cook for 5 minutes, stirring all the while with a wooden spoon.

Have a pint of the water ready in a jug. Add it slowly to the pan, stirring all the time so as to make a smooth mixture with the flour. Once mixed, add the rest of the water, the crumbled stock cube, paprika, mustard and molasses. Turn up the heat and bring to the boil.

Once boiling, reduce the heat and simmer for 30 minutes.

Before serving, sprinkle with finely chopped parsley. Serve garnished with croutons.

# stews

When On The Eighth Day first decided to open a Café in a corner of the whole food shop, one of the first utensils they bought was an ex-Army cast iron stew pot. It is still in use today - six gallon capacity and extremely solid, as anyone who has washed it up will testify. As well as building up the muscles and contributing to many a bad back, it has been the backbone of Café cuisine. It's full body producing many years of full bodied stews. We have selected some of the favourites for this book. Like the soups, they are all vegan and rely on pulses and slow cooking to thicken them.

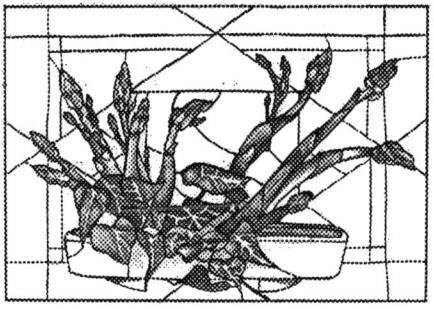

# caribbean stew

*The first recipe in this section has been made by us, in one form or another, for the last ten years. Its popularity is partly because it is tasty and interesting to cook, but also because the blend of peanut and coconut, with the spice of the chilli pepper, lifts it completely out of the everyday. To obtain the full benefit, turn up the gas fire, put on the Bermuda shorts, sip a glass of rum and get a loved one to hit you on the back of the head with a coconut. What bliss. Serves 4.*

- 8 oz (225g) dried kidney beans
- 1 lb (450g) potatoes - sweet potatoes if you can get them
- 1 red pepper
- 1 green pepper
- 8 oz (225g) frozen sweetcorn
- 3 cloves garlic
- 1 small fresh green or red chilli
- 1 large onion
- 1 cup orange juice
- 1 packet (4oz, 100g) creamed coconut
- 1 heaped tablespoon peanut butter
- dash Spanish paprika
- dash cayenne pepper
- handful fresh parsley
- 2 tablespoons sunflower oil
- pinch of salt and black pepper

Soak the beans overnight in cold water. Drain, rinse and cover with fresh water in a large pan. Bring to the boil and allow to boil vigorously for ten minutes, then simmer until soft. If you forget to soak them don't panic, they will cook, but will take at least an hour, possibly longer. You can substitute a 14oz (400g) can of red kidney beans in a real emergency!

While the beans cook, wash and peel the potatoes, just scrub them if they are organic. Dice into roughly one inch pieces and cook in a separate pan, until they are only just done.

Peel and roughly chop the onion and cook in the sunflower oil, in a large heavy bottomed pan. Stir occasionally to prevent sticking.

Cut the chilli in half lengthways and, unless you like hot food, remove the seeds. Peel the garlic and blend it and the chilli together, using a little sunflower oil if necessary. If you have not got a blender, finely chop the chilli and garlic. In any event add the chilli and garlic to the onions and continue to cook over a moderate heat.

Wash and roughly chop the peppers. Once the onions have cooked to softness, add them to the pan along with the paprika, cayenne pepper, salt and black pepper. Stir all together and allow to cook slowly. Meanwhile blend the coconut, peanut butter and orange juice together and then add to the pan. If you have no blender or are overcome with kitchen ennui, just add them to the pan separately. They will melt in eventually.

Once the sauce in the pan has come back to the simmer, add the sweetcorn and leave to cook.

Wash the parsley and chop it finely. When the sweetcorn and other ingredients are cooked, add the cooked potatoes, beans and chopped parsley. Stir everything together, adding a little water if necessary.

The result should be stew with quite a thick consistency and a hint of chilli. If, upon mature consideration, you decide you want it hotter next time, do not de-seed the chilli, or use two, or do both.

# hungarian goulash

*This is another recipe that has been re-invented by every new cook that has ever worked in the Café, and is none the worse for that. The current style has been modified for home consumption and makes for a good solid winter warmer. The only Hungarian who worked at Eighth Day was nonplussed by the suggestion that her countrywomen spent their time stuffing huge platefuls of this down themselves. Mind you she denied the existence of goulash as a national dish. Never ones to let the truth stand in the way of a good story, we present...*
*Serves 4.*

- 4 large potatoes (sweet potatoes are nice if you can get them)
- 1 large green pepper
- 4 oz (100g) mushrooms
- 2 cloves garlic
- 1 onion
- 1 tin (14oz, 400g) tomatoes
- 1 tablespoon Hungarian paprika (not Spanish paprika, it is not strong enough)
- 1 tablespoon tomato purée
- 1 desertspoon red grape juice
- 1 tablespoon sunflower oil
- good pinch of salt and pepper

First of all put on your oven to pre-heat to 200°C, 400°F, gas mark 6.

Peel and then finely chop the onion. Put the sunflower oil in a heavy bottomed casserole dish and heat on a medium light, adding the onion when hot. Cook for a few minutes, stirring occasionally.

Whilst the onion is cooking peel and crush the garlic and add to the pan.

Either blend the tinned tomatoes, with their juice, or chop them as small as you can. Add to the pan along with the tomato purée, paprika, juice, salt and pepper.

Wipe the mushrooms with a damp cloth or piece of kitchen towel. If large, cut into mouth size pieces, and add to the pan.

Scrub the potatoes, peel if not organic, and chop into large pieces. Add the potato to the casserole dish, mix well, adding a little water if it is too thick. It needs to be a fairly runny mixture at this stage, as it will thicken during the cooking. Cover the casserole and put it in the pre-heated oven.

Cook for about 1 hour until the potatoes are well done.

If you want to spoil yourself add a glass of red wine instead of the grape juice. It is possible to extend the cooking time by several hours if you keep the oven temperature down to 160°C (325°F), gas mark 3.

For a quicker method cook the potatoes separately and add to the rest of the mixture. You can then either finish it on top of the stove, or for only 30 minutes in the oven, or 10 minutes in the microwave on full power.

# tofu mattar paneer

*Most cooks, at some time or another, have to make a curry, just to show they can. Here at Eighth Day we tend to follow the method established by a cook from north west India, who left a fund of culinary skills but made off with the takings. Well, no one is perfect. At least the curry always works perfectly. This first curry is our vegan version of that old favourite Mattar Paneer. We replace the paneer cheese with tofu, it is simple to make and is one of the tastier things to do with a block of tofu. Serves 4.*

1 medium onion
1 lb (450g) small potatoes
1 lb (450g) frozen peas (mattar)
1 block (10oz, 275g) plain tofu
1 tin (14oz, 400g) tomatoes
1 small bunch fresh coriander
1 teaspoon mustard seed
1 teaspoon coriander seed
1 teaspoon black onion seed
1 clove garlic
1 inch (2.5 cm) piece of root ginger
1 chilli pepper
2 teaspoons ground cumin
1 teaspoon ground coriander
1 teaspoon turmeric
salt and pepper
sunflower oil

Wash the potatoes, peeling them if not organic. Cut them into bite sized pieces and put into a pan with just enough water to cover. With the lid on the pan to save energy, put on a high light until boiling, then reduce the heat to a good simmer. Leave to cook.

Put a heavy bottomed pan on a high light and add enough sunflower oil to just cover the bottom. Whilst it is heating, peel and roughly chop the onion and keep to one side. Put the mustard, coriander and onion seeds ready in a saucer, jar lid or other suitable receptacle. When the oil is smoking hot throw in the seeds and immediately cover the pan and turn down the light. The seeds will pop furiously. Leave them until the rate of popping slows but only for about half a minute and then put in the onions.

Stir the onions for a moment or two, to stop them burning and to take some of the heat out of the pan. Leave off the pan lid and let the onions continue to fry, while you peel and roughly chop the garlic. Wash or peel and chop the ginger. Wash and chop the chilli. Blend the garlic, chilli and ginger to a paste using a little oil if necessary. If you have not got a blender, or a mortar and pestle, do not worry, just chop them as finely as you can. Once processed, add them to the onions and stir. A word here about the chilli. Most of the heat in a chilli is in the seeds. If you want a milder flavour, de-seed the chilli. They also vary tremendously in flavour and heat, some of the hottest being the smallest. Only practice will teach you which is which.

Add the powdered spices to the pan and stir well, allowing the onions and paste to cook for a little while but not to burn.

Cube the block of tofu into one inch cubes. Add it to the pan and stir gently into the spice mixture, so it absorbs the flavour but does not break up.

Once the tofu has had a chance to get a nice spicy crust on it (about five or ten minutes) add the tin of tomatoes, roughly chopping them up either in the can or after you have got them in the pan. Stir the mixture well to blend all together and let it come back to the boil, making sure it does not stick. When the mixture is boiling, add the frozen peas and stir. Cover the pan and allow to come back to the boil.

Whilst waiting for the curry to boil, wash and chop the coriander leaves, discarding the stalks. Check on the potatoes and if cooked drain and, once the mixture has got back to a simmer, add them to the curry along with the coriander. Obviously if the potatoes are not cooked wait until they are! Mix all together and allow to cook for as long as possible, (at least five minutes) even if you are starving, to allow all the flavours to blend.

Serve with rice and raita.

# raita

- Piece of cucumber, about two inches (50mm) long
- 1 large tub yoghurt
- 1 clove garlic
- 2 teaspoons mint
- salt and pepper

Crush or very finely chop the garlic.

Empty the yoghurt into a suitable bowl and add the garlic, mint and a pinch of salt and pepper. Chop the cucumber into small dice and add to the yoghurt stirring it well to mix. Serve as an accompaniment to any curry.

# chick pea & aubergine curry

*The second curry in the collection is another long established favourite, made in various modes by succeeding generations of Eighth Day cooks. This version makes a curry that varies from hot to hellish, depending on chilli content. If you are unsure of your tolerance, start off with less rather than more. If you overdo it, don't pour water down your throat as this does not help at all. Eat a bit of rice or bread and put that Ravi Shankar CD on to get you into the mood. Serves 4 - 6.*

- 1 large onion
- 10 oz (300g) chick peas.
- 1 large aubergine
- 2 inch (5cm) piece of root ginger
- 2 cloves garlic
- 2-6 fresh chillies
- 1 tin (14oz, 400g) tomatoes
- 4 oz (100g) tomato purée
- 1/4 pint (125ml) tomato juice
- 2 teaspoons cumin seeds
- 2 teaspoons brown mustard seeds
- 2 teaspoon ground cumin
- 2 teaspoons ground coriander
- 2 teaspoons ground turmeric
- 1 teaspoon ground fenugreek
- 1/2 teaspoon cayenne pepper
- 1 bunch fresh coriander

Soak the chick peas overnight in cold water. Drain, rinse and put in a saucepan. Cover with cold water and cook on a high light. When boiling turn down to a simmer, cover and allow to cook. Chick peas may take up to an hour to cook, so it is best to give yourself plenty of time. The good news is that you cannot overcook them even if you try.

Put your heaviest pan on a high light and add enough oil to cover the bottom. Put all the seeds in a saucer or other vessel and whilst the oil is heating, peel and chop the onion. When the oil smokes, throw in the seeds, cover the pan and shake it a little to get the seeds really popping. Turn down the heat and, as soon as the initial explosion is over, put in the onions, stirring so they do not burn.

Wash the ginger and chillies, peel the garlic and crush or blend them to a smooth paste, using a little oil if necessary. As with the previous recipe, just finely chop everything if you are without the benefit of a blender. Add the paste to the onion mixture and allow to cook for five minutes or so, making sure it does not stick.

Add all the rest of the spices, except the fresh coriander, and carry on cooking, stirring well to prevent burning.

Wash the aubergine and cut into fairly large dice or slices and add to the pan. Leave to cook for ten minutes.

Blend or chop the tinned tomato and add to the pan, along with the purée and the tomato juice. Mix it all together and leave to continue cooking.

Once the chick peas are cooked, drain, rinse well and add to the pan. Stir the curry together and season to taste. Cover and allow to simmer slowly for 30 minutes adding water if necessary.

Wash and chop the fresh coriander and add to the curry. Stir in and serve immediately.

Here at Eighth Day, we tend to cook all our stews on top of the stove because it is easier for us to handle the large quantities we produce. At home though there is no reason why you have to, so this curry for example could be left in the oven to finish once all the ingredients are in the dish.

# japanese kimpira stew

*Now, from the land of the rising sun, no, we do not mean Yorkshire, we bring you a stew redolent of all the exotic flavours of the orient. Sorry about the purple prose but we really like this stew! There is an ancient Japanese story about Kimpira, something to do with the strength of the sauce giving humans the strength to fight bears. We would recite it here but we have forgotten it - just as well really as the following stew bears no relation to the traditional Japanese sauce. The cook who invented it just pinched the name. Well, it's better than pinching the recipe. Serves 4 - 6.*

- 1 large onion
- 2 cloves garlic
- 2 inch (5cm) piece of fresh root ginger
- 2 tablespoons shoyu
- 2 tablespoons sesame oil
- 2 medium carrots
- 1 small swede
- 1 small cauliflower
- 1 oz (25g) mushrooms
- 2 courgettes
- 1 small head spring cabbage
- 1 small tin sweetcorn
- 1 packet (2oz, 50g) Arame
- 8 oz (225g) kidney beans
- 1 block plain tofu (optional)
- 1 sprig fresh parsley

Ideally the kidney beans should be washed and then soaked overnight in cold water, if you have forgotten to soak them they will cook from the dried state but will take ages. First take the soaked beans, rinse them and put in a pan with plenty of water and bring to the boil. Boil them fiercely for at least ten minutes then reduce the heat, cover and simmer until cooked.

Wash the carrots and swede, peeling if not organic, and the cauliflower. Break the cauliflower into florets and chop or slice into small batons or dice. Bring a large saucepan of water to the boil and blanch the carrot, swede and cauliflower for five minutes. Strain, reserving the vegetables and 17 fl oz (500ml) of the water.

Peel and chop the onion and keep to one side for a moment. Wash the ginger, peel the garlic and blend together in a little sunflower oil. If you have no blender, chop finely or crush. Put the resultant paste in a large (4 to 6 pint at least) heavy bottomed pan. Add the sesame oil and shoyu and put on a low heat. Add the chopped onion, the garlic and ginger paste and cook gently for five minutes.

While the onion mixture is cooking, wash the courgette and wipe over the mushrooms with a damp cloth. Slice the courgette and the mushrooms (if they are larger than button size) and add to the pan. Allow to cook for another five minutes then add the blanched vegetables and the water you saved.

Put the arame in a bowl, cover with boiling water, and allow to soak for five minutes. Mix into the stew, adding the soaking water if needed to thin it out.

Next wash and thinly slice the spring cabbage and add to the pan. Drain the sweetcorn and add, making sure you give the pan a good stir to mix all the ingredients.

Cover the pan and allow the stew to carry on cooking. Once the beans are cooked strain, rinse and add them to the pan, stirring well.

If you are using tofu, cube the block and add it to the pan. Wash and chop the parsley and add. Mix well and leave to simmer for 30 minutes. Season to taste and serve immediately.

The seaweed and ginger give this stew a unique flavour and you a rosy glow of inner fulfilment.

# mediterranean stew

This next recipe used to be the Café 'Teaching Stew', both because it is considered easy to make and was one of the few legible recipes we possessed at the time. All new workers made it as their first attempt at cooking and were only allowed to progress when they had mastered Mediterranean Stew. This proved to be a mixed blessing, as, although it is a simple recipe, and when made properly, both looks and tastes wonderful, some of the heroic failures turned out by learners ruined its reputation and it fell both out of favour and off the menu. Recently it has been rehabilitated and is just as satisfying as ever it was in it's heyday. Long standing customers may remember the following witty repartee:
Customer of sober mien, consulting menu: "What's in the Mediterranean?"
Eighth Day worker:
"Salty water with a slick of suntan oil"
Oh happy days!
Serves 4 - 6.

8 oz (250g) black eye beans
8 oz (250g) black olives
2 oz (50g) mushrooms
1 small aubergine
3 medium carrots
2 courgettes
4 sticks celery
½ spring cabbage
1 large onion
2 cloves garlic
5 oz (125g) tomato purée
2 teaspoons basil
2 teaspoons mint
1 tin (14oz, 400g) tomatoes
½ pint (300ml) tomato juice
½ pint (250ml) red grape juice
3 tablespoons wine vinegar
2 tablespoons olive oil
salt and pepper

Soak the beans overnight in cold water, rinse, cover with water in a pan and bring to the boil. Leave to simmer until cooked. Black Eyed Beans are among the quickest to cook, so there is no need to panic if you have not soaked them. Just wash well and boil, they will be ready in under an hour.

Peel the onion and chop or slice into medium pieces. Peel, crush or chop the garlic, or blend it in a little olive oil. Put a large pan on a medium light.

Add the olive oil, garlic and onion and allow to cook gently. If you are using dried herbs, add them now and allow to cook for five minutes. If you are lucky enough to have fresh herbs, wash and chop them and add to the onions after five minutes.

Meanwhile wash and peel your vegetables as necessary, make sure to peel the carrots if they are not organic. Slice the celery and courgette, not too thinly, and add to the onions.

Cut the aubergine lengthways into four and then chop into bite size pieces, add to the pan and stir the contents round to help cook evenly. Leave to cook for a further five minutes.

Chop the carrot into small sections or julienne and add to pan, stirring occasionally to prevent burning.

Blend or chop the tinned tomatoes and add to the pan along with the tomato purée, fruit juice, vinegar and seasoning. Mix well together, cover and continue to cook slowly.

Whilst the beans finish cooking, wash and shred the spring cabbage.

When the beans are cooked, drain them, rinse and add to the pan with the cabbage and olives, mixing everything together. If you do not stone the olives, please warn your guests, unless you are on commission from a dentist. If necessary thin the stew with water and adjust the seasoning.

Allow to simmer for a further 20 to 30 minutes until all the flavours are blended.

This is another dish that benefits from a nice glass of red wine - half in the stew and half in the cook of course!

# salads

*In the early years of Eighth Day, we only ever produced one Salad, the ubiquitous green, served with the famous Eighth Day salad dressing. This daily salad was made in huge quantities and, although it did make it easier to choose which salad to have, eventually became too boring for the staff, let alone the customers. With the advent of a better chilled counter, we were able to produce more salads, eventually settling down to four a day. Since then we have gone salad mad! Most of our salads are fairly substantial concoctions - none of your limp lettuce for us. Here are some of the favourites, all quick and simple to make but ideal accompaniments to a main course or snack or on their own for really healthy eating.*

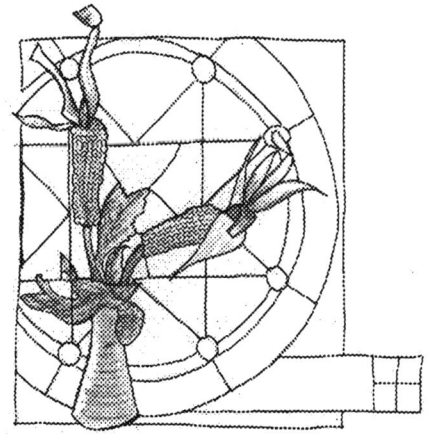

# spicy kidney bean salad

*The first Salad has become a firm favourite. It goes very well with barbecued food and eastern dishes and is a good winter salad. Serves 4.*

½ lb red kidney beans
3 medium tomatoes
½ cauliflower
2 teaspoons cumin seeds
½ lemon
 sprig parsley
 olive oil
 salt and pepper

Wash the beans and soak over night in cold water. Rinse and cover with fresh water in a pan. Bring to the boil and keep boiling vigorously for at least ten to fifteen minutes to destroy the toxins that exist in these beans. Then turn down the heat and allow to cook until tender.

Whilst the beans are cooking, cut the half cauliflower into small florets, wash and leave to drain in a sieve or colander.

Next heat the oil in a wok or heavy pan and add the cumin seeds. Keep stirring the seeds until they are fried to a nice golden brown and begin to pop. Make sure they do not burn. Once the seeds are cooked, add the cauliflower and mix well letting it cook until just done, remove from the heat immediately and allow to cool.

Keep an eye on those beans, and as soon as they are cooked, drain, rinse well with plenty of cold water, and allow to cool.

Wash the tomatoes and cut them into wedges. Rinse the parsley and chop it finely. Squeeze the lemon making sure to sieve out the pips.

Mix all the ingredients together carefully seasoning to taste with a little salt and pepper. The dried kidney beans can, of course, be replaced with a tin of ready cooked beans. Just rinse them well to remove the liquid, which always tastes horrible.

# rice salad á la quay co-op

*This recipe was one of a job lot imported from Cork City in Ireland, along with a cook, or was it the other way round? In any event it is another winner, and like the previous one, it is good all year round but particularly useful in winter when salad vegetables are at a premium. The combination of spices and shoyu give it a decidedly oriental flavour. Serves 4.*

- 4 oz (100g) cooked brown rice
- 2 oz (50g) roasted peanuts
- 1 large leek
- 2 teaspoons dry ginger powder
- 3 tablespoons shoyu
- 2 teaspoons turmeric
- sunflower oil

Trim the leek. Thinly slice and wash to remove any grit, then drain well.

Put a little sunflower oil in a Wok on a fairly high heat. Add the leek and the ginger and fry, stirring constantly for two minutes. Add the turmeric and fry for one more minute.

Add the shoyu and stir well together for half a minute, then remove from heat and allow to cool. When the leek mixture has cooled, mix with the rice and peanuts.

If you have not got roasted peanuts, use plain peanuts and roast them yourself. Put the nuts on a baking tray, drizzle a little sunflower oil on them and put them in a hot oven. Check them after five minutes and, as soon as they are browned, take them out and cool. Alternatively you can roast them on top of the stove, in a heavy frying pan, cast iron is best, using very little oil.

If you are in a mood to be generous, smoked tofu compliments the leek and ginger very well. Either include a little in the salad or serve braised, smoked tofu with it as a starter.

If you ever find yourself in Cork, call in at the Quay Co-op's Café, they are a good crowd of fellow co-operators and at the mention of our name, will probably overcharge you!

# beetroot & apple salad

*The flavours of beetroot and apple seem to go so well together that it is a surprise more dishes do not contain the combination. Granny Smith apples do very nicely or failing that, any firm greenish apple, avoid the ghastly Golden Delicious if you can. Serves 4.*

4 small cooked beetroot
2 tablespoons toasted sesame seeds
3 green apples
1 carrot
2 pineapple rings - optional
1 large sprig parsley
French dressing

Toast the sesame seeds, either on a tray in a hot oven, or in a heavy pan on top of the stove, until they go light brown. Be careful not to burn them.

Wash, core and slice the apples into thin wedges.

We have presumed that you will use ready processed beetroot, the sort that come in vacuum packs. If you are using fresh beetroot, just scrub them and boil in plenty of water to which you have added a couple of tablespoons of vinegar. This helps to keep the colour from bleeding out. When they are cooked let them cool, the skin will peel off in your fingers.

Chop the beetroot into small dice. Cut the pineapple into small wedges.

Peel the carrot and grate finely.

Wash, drain and finely chop the parsley.

Mix well together and then add eight tablespoons of French dressing, either shop bought, or as follows.

# french dressing

6 tablespoons olive oil
2 tablespoon white wine or cider vinegar
¼ teaspoon of French or Dijon mustard
pinch of mixed herbs
pinch of salt

Mix all together and blend or put in a clean jam jar, screw on the lid and shake vigorously.

# broccoli & orange salad

*Another simple salad using just a few carefully selected ingredients that will enhance any menu. Serves 4.*

1 large head broccoli
2 carrots
3 large oranges
2 oz toasted sunflower seeds
8 tablespoons French dressing- made with sesame oil
the juice of half an orange

Toast the sunflower seeds as described in the previous recipe.

Wash and chop the broccoli lengthways, leaving as much stalk as possible.

Peel and grate the carrot. Peel the orange and remove the inner skin from the individual segments. This is best done with a small, very sharp knife with the peeled orange whole. Cut down between the skin and the orange segment. You will find the flesh of the orange comes away without breaking. Discard the pips and cut each segment into halves.

Mix all the ingredients together carefully, adding the orange juice.

Make French dressing as shown in the previous recipe but use sesame oil instead of the olive oil and omit the mustard. Add to the salad and mix to coat all the ingredients. The sesame oil lifts this salad quite out of the ordinary and adds that certain something to the differing textures of crunchy broccoli and juicy orange.

# chickpea peasant salad

*This salad is a variant of the traditional Greek salad so common around the eastern Mediterranean. It uses the usual tomato and feta but has the addition of chick peas and watercress to lift it to new heights. Serves 4.*

- 8 oz (225g) chick peas
- 1 onion
- 1 clove garlic
- 3 tomatoes
- 1 red pepper
- 2 bunches watercress
- 1 tablespoon chopped parsley
- 8 tablespoons French dressing
- 4 oz (100g) feta cheese - optional

Wash and soak the chick peas overnight. Rinse and put in a pan. Cover with water and bring to the boil. Once boiling, turn down the heat and simmer, with the pan covered, until they are cooked. This could be at least an hour. Once the chick peas are cooked, remove from the heat, strain and rinse with plenty of cold water and leave to cool.

Peel and chop the onion finely and mix with the cooked chick peas. Wash and drain the pepper, tomatoes, watercress and parsley.

Cut the pepper into two lengthways. Pull out the seeds and white pith from the end and discard. Cut each half pepper into medium slices across the width and then into halves again down the length.

Coarsely chop the watercress. Cut the tomatoes into wedges and finely chop the parsley. Finely chop the garlic. Make French dressing as in the recipe for Beetroot and Apple Salad and add the garlic and blend. If you have not got a blender just add the chopped garlic to the dressing anyway.

When ready to serve, mix everything together and add the cubed feta cheese.

You can vary this by using the juice of a lemon and a good dollop of olive oil instead of the French dressing. Add the chopped garlic to the other ingredients in the mixture before adding the lemon juice and oil. Garnish with some chopped oregano and thinly sliced lemon.

# italian pasta salad

*Dream of Italy while you make and eat the next delicious salad. As soon as the smell of fresh basil drifts round the kitchen, you will suddenly find yourself the centre of attention. Well, it's one way of getting a social life. Serves 4.*

- 8 oz (225g) pasta spirals
- 3 tomatoes
- 4 oz (100g) fresh spinach
- 2 oz (50g) fresh basil leaves
- 3 sprigs parsley
- 1 clove garlic
- ½ lemon
- 3 floz (75ml) olive oil
- salt and black pepper

Put a large pan, half full of water, on to boil and add a pinch of salt. When boiling put in the pasta and boil vigorously until just cooked. Drain immediately, rinse with cold water and drain again. Then put into a bowl with a little olive oil and stir gently until coated. This will stop the pasta sticking together.

Wash the spinach thoroughly, chop coarsely and add it to the cooked pasta.

Wash and quarter the tomatoes. Add to the mix.

**Now make the dressing.**

Juice the lemon and mix the juice with the olive oil, garlic, parsley, half the basil leaves, salt and pepper. Blend until smooth.

Add the dressing to the salad, mix it all gently together and sprinkle 1oz of roughly chopped basil leaves on top as a garnish.

This is so easy to make and yet has such an intensive flavour. It is marvellous eaten just with ciabatta bread and rough, red wine.

# mediterranean rice salad

*Here is another lemon vinaigrette based recipe which is as tasty and satisfying as a risotto, which it very nearly is. Make this one with your barbecues, but make a lot! Serves 4.*

- 8 oz (225g) long grain, brown rice
- 1 red pepper
- 1 green pepper
- 4 spring onions
- 2 tomatoes
- 8 black olives
- 2 tablespoons parsley
- 1 clove garlic
- ½ lemon
- 3 floz (75ml) olive oil
- salt and black pepper

Wash, rinse and cook the rice. Drain and rinse in cold water, and allow to cool.

Wash the other vegetables, de-seed the peppers and slice them thinly. Cut the tomatoes into wedges. Finely chop the spring onion and parsley. Pit the black olives. If you have not got a pitter, slice them in half and remove the stone that way.

Mix all the prepared vegetables with the cooked rice.

Squeeze the lemon, strain the pips out of the juice and mix it with the olive oil, salt and black pepper. Peel and chop the garlic and add it to the mixture. Blend until smooth and pour on to the salad, stirring it gently to coat the ingredients.

The dressings we have used in our recipes, can all be made in larger quantities and kept refrigerated for up to three days. If they separate out, just blend them or shake them again. You will have noticed that the preceding two salads use a similar dressing, so you could make one batch of the basic recipe, in advance and add the basil and parsley to half, just before serving. Two summer party salads, with half the work.

# on the 8th day salad dressing

*Finally, by popular request, the recipe for the world famous On The Eighth Day salad dressing. We have produced this dressing for as long as anyone can remember and no-one has any idea of its origins. It works every time and is fantastic and wonderful, especially on salad!*

17 fl oz (500ml) sunflower oil
5 fl oz (150ml) cider vinegar
1 medium onion
1 tablespoon tomato purée
1 tablespoon Eighth Day salad dressing mix (buy it from our shop)
3.5 floz (100ml) soya milk

Peel and chop the onion and mix with all the ingredients except the soya milk. Blend into a smooth liquid and with the blender running, add the soya milk slowly until the mixture thickens. The dressing will keep for three days in the refrigerator.

# bakes

To those readers who are not customers of the Café, the heading of this section is apt to be confusing. For as long as we have run the Café, the style of the menu has been roughly the same. We make a fresh soup, a fresh stew and another main course, which is always finished off in the oven, and so has acquired the generic name of 'Bake'. These dishes involve a bit more work than the average soup or stew and often need a separate sauce as an accompaniment. Complete novices should perhaps wait until a couple of stews have been mastered before attempting a bake.

Over the years it has been the bakes that have seen the most innovation, especially in the days when we had no menu planning at all. The individual cooks just pleased themselves what they made. In fact there was a time when one of our cooks vowed never to repeat a recipe twice. Every day was a voyage into the unknown!

Now we are much less adventurous - to the relief of the poor customers, it must be said - but we still make dishes discovered by those culinary alchemists. And delicious they are too. So, take your oven dishes and baking trays and explore the heritage of the Eighth Day Bake.

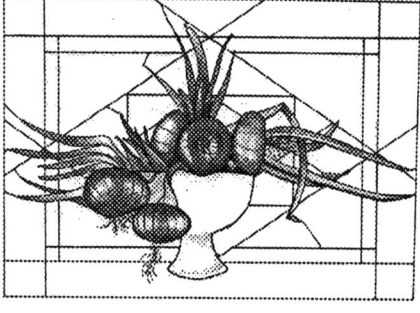

# cauliflower & lentil bake

*The origins of this first recipe are lost in the mists of time. In fact we would not be surprised to find a tray of it in the next tomb of a Pharaoh to be discovered. Like nearly all of the previous dishes, it has gone through many stages of development. The original was made without a white sauce but, these days, it never is. As old hands will know, eventually the wheel will turn full circle and a new generation of cooks will decide it is far superior if the sauce is missed out! Either way it is a fine example of the traditional, Eighth Day, whole food style of cookery and although simple, is simply delicious. It can be made vegan or dairy based, both versions are given, just miss out the cheese and milk. Serves 4 - 6.*

1 lb (450g) red lentils
2 onions
   dash of shoyu
2 small or 1 large cauliflower

**For the sauce**
1 pint (600ml) milk - cows or soya
1 oz (25g) butter or margarine
1 oz (25g) wholemeal flour
1 teaspoon whole grain mustard
   pinch of nutmeg
   pinch of black pepper
   pinch of salt

**Topping**
8 oz (225g) bread crumbs
   sunflower oil
8 oz (225g) cheese - grated, or 1 block smoked tofu - chopped small

Wash and rinse the lentils well and place in a good sized, preferably heavy bottomed pan. Cover with cold water and add a good dash of shoyu (up to a dessertspoon full). Put on a medium heat until boiling. Stir occasionally to make sure they do not stick. Once boiling turn down the heat and cover. Leave to simmer until cooked. Check from time to time, to make sure they do not stick and burn. Add a little water if they dry out but not so much that they turn into a complete mush!

Peel and thinly slice the onions and fry until soft in a little sunflower oil with a pinch of black pepper. Once soft, keep to one side.

Remove and discard any damaged leaves from the cauliflower, thinly shred the remaining leaves. Cut the cauliflower into small florets and wash with the leaves.

Half fill a medium sized pan with water and bring to the boil. When boiling, add the cauliflower and cook for five minutes. Drain and put to one side.

To make the white sauce, first put the milk on a low heat but don't let it boil. Whilst it is heating, follow the other steps.

Melt the butter or margarine in a small but heavy pan. Add the flour and cook for a few minutes, stirring continuously.

Slowly add the hot milk, stirring all the while to prevent lumps forming. The sauce will thicken almost instantly. Add the mustard and nutmeg to the sauce, mix and bring back to the boil, stirring all the time. If, despite your attention, lumps do form, give the sauce a good beating with a whisk, or blend it. Some cooks prefer to do the whole operation with a whisk in the first place. In any event, once the sauce has come to the boil, remove from the heat and season to taste.

Mix the bread crumbs and cheese or tofu in a suitable bowl. Then add a little sunflower oil until the mixture is evenly oiled. Make sure not to overdo the oil, as it only needs to be moist.

Add the onions to the cooked lentils and mix well. Put the mixture in an even layer in the bottom of an ovenproof dish.

Place the cooked cauliflower in a layer on top of the lentils. Pour the sauce over the cauliflower and sprinkle the bread crumb mixture over the top.

Bake in a moderate oven for 30 minutes at: gas mark 5, 190ºC, 375ºF.

To make the original version of this recipe, take everything as above except the white sauce.

Add the mustard to the bread crumb mix, before adding the oil. Layer the dish in the same way, finishing with the bread crumb and cheese. This makes for a slightly drier meal but just as tasty and even easier to prepare. You pays your money and you makes your choice. The important thing is the taste of lentils, shoyu and cauliflower - one of the great culinary discoveries of all time.

# pea pie with mushroom gravy

*Now this recipe is a classic of the traditional 'good solid food' school of cookery. Pies are our English heritage and our gift to the world's cuisine. At least real 'rib lining' pies are ! None of your namby-pamby, melt in the mouth morsels for our ancestors - great wedges of pie for them, with scores of local variations. You knew where you were with the pies in those days.*

*This is a Lancashire pie, it must be because it contains that ambrosia of the Cotton Towns, mushy peas! So tuck in to this, but make sure you tuck in the duvet afterwards.*
*Serves 4.*

**Pastry**
4 oz (100g) self-raising wholemeal flour
2 oz (50g) margarine
1 to 2 tablespoons water
pinch salt

**Filling**
1 small medium onion
½ teaspoon sage
salt and pepper
8 oz (225g) marrowfat peas
12 oz (350g) potatoes
1 small carrot
sunflower oil

**Sauce**
4 oz (100g) mushrooms
3 tablespoons soya sauce
1 tablespoon flour
½ onion
½ pint (300ml) vegetable stock
salt and pepper
sunflower oil

Soak the peas overnight in plenty of cold water. Next day, drain them, rinse and put into a suitable sized pan. Cover with water and bring to the boil. When boiling put the lid on the pan and simmer until completely soft - mushy but not liquid!

Start making the pastry by mixing the flour, margarine and salt in a mixing bowl. Using your fingertips, mix until left with a breadcrumb-like consistency. Add the cold water a little at a time, as you knead to make a stiff but pliable dough. Once the dough is evenly mixed, set aside in a cool place or in the fridge, to rest until wanted.

Now make the filling. There is plenty of time because those peas are going to be ages before they cook. So first of all wash the potatoes, peel if they are not organic, and cut into medium dice. Put them in a pan and cover with salted water and cook until soft. Drain and put to one side.

Peel and chop up the onion quite finely and fry in a little sunflower oil with the sage and a pinch of salt and pepper. When the onion is soft and golden, remove from the heat and set aside.

Scrub the carrot, peel if it is not organic, and grate it finely.

When the peas are cooked, drain, saving the liquor. Mix the onion, peas, potatoes and grated carrot and place in a pie dish. Use some of the pea water to moisten the mixture if it seems too dry.

Working on a floured surface, roll out the pastry to fit the dish. Trim, tuck in the edges, and make a cut in the top to let out the steam. Brush with a trace of sunflower oil.

Bake in a moderate oven, gas mark 5, 190°C, 375°F, for 40 to 45 minutes. Check after 30 minutes, do not let the crust burn.

Whilst the pie is in the oven, make the gravy.

Peel and chop the onion finely. Heat a little sunflower oil in a pan and add the onion, Wipe the mushrooms with a kitchen towel and chop them finely. Add to the onions and allow to cook until they start to loose their moisture, then add the shoyu and a pinch of salt and pepper.

Stir in the flour and cook on for 5 minutes, stirring all the while. Add the stock, bring to the boil and simmer for 10 minutes. Blend if you prefer a smooth sauce.

If you have a pressure cooker you can cook the peas without soaking. It is really better to soak as marrowfats can be like bullets. Many people ask us the secret of nice pastry. It is a bit like making cakes, some people just cannot do it. For most of us however it seems to come down to three things: First, use cold water, not lukewarm. Second, have cold hands. Third, do not spend much time on it. The longer you mess around with pastry, the more it will resemble cardboard when you cook it. The moral; good pastry cooks are cold people with a short attention span.

# béchamel sauce

Some of the following recipes depend on a proper béchamel sauce to be truly mouth watering, so to simplify matters, we will give the recipe for the basic sauce now, rather than repeat ourselves. Béchamel is really what us plebs call white sauce, but it is far tastier than the hot wallpaper paste which many cooks serve up.

- 1 pint (600ml) milk (dairy or soya)
- 1 oz (25g) butter or margarine
- 1 oz (25g) plain flour
- 1 small onion or a piece the size of a walnut
- 1 bay leaf
- 1 sprig fresh thyme or a pinch of dried thyme
- 1 pinch fresh ground black pepper
- 1 pinch fresh grated nutmeg
- 1 pinch salt

First melt the butter in a saucepan, over a low light. When melted, add the flour and stir well with a wooden spoon, until you have a smooth paste - this is a roux.

Cook the roux for two or three minutes, stirring continuously. Then add the milk in three or four stages, stirring each addition in to prevent lumps.

Once the milk is all added and the sauce is smooth, add the onion, bay leaf and thyme. Bring slowly to the boil and simmer gently for about 10 minutes, stirring occasionally to prevent sticking.

Strain the sauce though a sieve into a suitable jug or other container and add the nutmeg, salt and pepper to taste.

This basic sauce can be made beforehand and kept covered, in the fridge, for up to 3 days. Some cooks put in a small piece of celery and carrot with the onion, some use a sachet of bouquet garni instead of the bay leaf and thyme, some use a bit of marjoram and rosemary - it's not fixed in stone so play around until you find your favourite method. We hope you like the genuine French terminology creeping into the text. Do a bit of posing and impress your friends.

# butter bean bake

The second recipe is another from the antique collection, as our more antique customers will recognise. This one really does need a proper béchamel for perfection, so take your time with the sauce - it's worth the effort. Serves 4.

**Base**
14 oz (400g) tin butter beans or 7oz (200g) dried butter beans
1 medium onion
1 tablespoon olive oil
8 oz (225g) carrots
1 medium cauliflower
2 tablespoons shoyu
salt

1 ½ quantities (1 ½ pints, 900ml) béchamel sauce, see page 47
1 dessertspoon fresh parsley

**Topping**
6 oz (175g) breadcrumbs
4 floz (125ml) olive oil
2 oz (50g) grated cheese or vegan cheese substitute

Dried beans need to be soaked overnight, rinsed and boiled in fresh water for about 40 minutes, until soft. If you use tinned beans rinse the contents and drain before using.

Whilst the beans are cooking, peel and finely dice the onion and sauté in a teaspoon of olive oil in a heavy bottomed pan. Once soft, remove from the heat and keep on one side.

Peel and chop the carrots into sticks, or, if you have a food processor, julienne them. Bring some water to the boil in a medium sized pan. Put in the carrot and boil until partly cooked, reserve the water.

Break the cauliflower up into florets. Wash, drain, then boil in the carrot water, being careful not to overcook - the florets should remain firm. Once cooked drain and reserve.

Now make $1\frac{1}{2}$ times the quantity of the béchamel sauce recipe given above. Use $1\frac{1}{2}$ pints (900ml) milk, $1\frac{1}{2}$ oz (40g) butter and $1\frac{1}{2}$ oz (40g) flour, then follow the instructions. Once made, add the fresh chopped parsley.

Grate the cheese, mix with the bread crumbs and 4 floz (125ml) of olive oil to make the topping.

Drain the beans and mix with the sautéed onion, shoyu and salt (to taste). Place in the bottom of an oven proof dish.

Layer on the cooked carrots and then the cauliflower. Pour the béchamel sauce over the top and finally sprinkle on the topping.

Bake in a moderate oven for 30 minutes at: gas mark 5, 190°C, 375°F.

Obviously to make a vegan version use the vegan ingredients - it is just as good either way. You can use any proprietary brand of vegan 'cheese' that you prefer, or miss it out and just use breadcrumbs, oil and a good pinch of paprika.

# filo pie with tomato & coriander sauce

*Here is the second pie in the collection. This time it is about as far removed from traditional Manchester cookery as you can get. No need to worry about making the pastry either, as it uses sheets of filo - that delicate crust from Greece and the eastern Mediterranean. The filling has much more to do with Mexico. Now that really is international cookery, half way around the globe in one dish. One similarity with the previous pie is the fact that it is vegan, although you can use dairy milk without any problem. Serves 4.*

**Filling**
14oz (400g) tin pinto beans or
7oz (200g) dried beans
1  medium onion
2  cloves garlic
   small bunch fresh coriander
2  medium courgettes
   small tin sweetcorn or 4oz (100g) frozen or fresh sweetcorn
1  block smoked tofu
   sunflower oil
   shoyu
1  pint (600ml) béchamel sauce, page 47
   pinch cayenne pepper
   pinch paprika

**The pastry top**
6 sheets filo pastry
blob of margarine

**Tomato & Coriander Sauce**
1  tin (14oz, 400g) tin tomatoes
1  small onion
1  clove garlic
   small bunch fresh coriander
¼  pint (150ml) tomato juice
   sunflower oil
   salt and pepper

Soak the pinto beans overnight if you can. Rinse and drain them, then cover with fresh water in a largish pan. Cover and bring to the boil. Allow to cook until soft, which will take about an hour. The beans will cook un-soaked fairly well if you forget to soak them but they will take a bit longer. Of course if you use a can, just rinse the contents and drain.

Let the filo pastry thaw out, either in the fridge or covered with a damp tea towel.

**To prepare the filling.**

Peel and finely chop the onion. Peel and crush the garlic. Put a little oil in a frying pan and heat on a medium light. Add the onion and garlic. Sauté until the onion is soft, then set aside in a mixing bowl.

Wash the courgettes, top and tail them. Cut into quarters lengthways, then chop into small chunks. Sauté in a little oil using the pan you cooked the onions in, but do not let them brown. After about five minutes add a dash of shoyu and cook on for a few minutes more to allow them to absorb the flavour and soften. Add to the mixing bowl.

Wash and drain the coriander. Chop coarsely and add to the mixing bowl.

If using a tin of sweetcorn, just drain the liquid, rinse and add the corn to the mixture in the bowl. Fresh or frozen corn should be cooked in enough boiling water to cover, or microwaved with a spot of water in a covered container. Add to the mixture.

Cube the block of tofu into smallish dice. Add the cooked beans and tofu to the mixture in the bowl. Stir all the ingredients together adding a good pinch of salt and pepper.

Now prepare the béchamel sauce, page 47, when cooked add the pinch of cayenne and paprika.

Take the filling mixture and put it in a shallow, oblong pie dish or tin and pour the sauce over it.

It is now ready to have the crust put on.

Preheat the oven to gas mark 4, 180°C, 350°F.

Prepare a small dish of melted margarine. If your pastry is not already covered with a damp tea towel take it out of it's packet and cover it with one now.

Unwrap the first sheet of filo and carefully lay it flat on a clean work surface. Gently brush the entire sheet with some of the melted margarine and lay the next sheet on top. Repeat until all the filo is layered in a neat stack. After you remove each sheet from the pack recover the rest or it will dry and be very brittle.

Place the complete pastry top over the pie filling and, either trim the edges to fit the pie dish or fold them under to fit! Some people find it easier to assemble the filo crust on a clean tea towel which can then be inverted onto the top of the pie. Pop the pie in the preheated oven for approximately 20 minutes until the pastry is crisp and pale brown in colour.

Whilst the pie is cooking, prepare the Tomato and Coriander Sauce.

Peel and finely chop the onion. Peel and crush the garlic and fry, with the onion, in a little oil until soft, then add the chopped tomatoes and tomato juice. Let it come to the boil then reduce the heat and simmer.

Wash the coriander, remove the stalks and finely chop before adding this to the sauce. Season to taste with salt and pepper. Allow to carry on cooking until the pie is ready to serve.

Try serving with rice and roasted red peppers or one of our salads. To roast peppers, just wash them, cut lengthways into wide slices, de-seed and put on a oven-proof tray. Drizzle on a little olive oil and roast in a hot oven gas mark 7, $220°C$, $425°F$ until they just start to burn, yummy.

# pasta arrabiata

*This is pasta with a difference - hot and fiery. The name suggests the East, but with the combination of chilli and oregano, it tastes more like a chilli from the new world. Mind you, if you keep going east you arrive in America eventually. Go easy on the chilli peppers at first unless you are a spice fan. Serves 4.*

10 oz (300g) fusilli or penne pasta
1 medium onion
2-3 cloves garlic
2-4 chilli peppers
6 oz (175g) mushrooms
1 green pepper
4 large spring cabbage leaves
1 tin (14oz 400g) tomatoes
½ pint (450ml) passata or tomato juice
6 oz (175g) grated cheese
1 level teaspoon basil
1 level teaspoon oregano
1 large pinch chilli powder
dash of red wine or red grape juice
salt and pepper
olive oil

Pre-heat the oven to gas mark 7, 220°C, 425°F.

Half fill a large pan with cold water and add a good shake of salt. Bring to the boil. Add the pasta, stir to make sure it is separated. Bring back to the boil and turn down the heat slightly so the water boils fairly vigorously. Partially cover and leave to cook for about 10 minutes until just soft or 'al dente'. As soon as it is cooked drain in a colander and then put it back into the hot pan to keep warm. If you are using fresh pasta, it will only take 3 minutes to cook. Some cooks add a dash of olive oil to the water before putting in the pasta to prevent it clumping together in the pan. If you use enough water you should not have a problem. You can add a dash to the cooked and drained pasta and stir it well. This will stop it sticking while it cools, and makes it smell delicious.

While the pasta is cooking, peel and chop the onion and set to one side. Peel the garlic. If you are a garlic lover, like most of us, use 3 cloves, in any event, chop it finely and set to one side.

Wash the chilli peppers (think carefully about how hot you like your food before you use three), then slice in two lengthways. Unless you like really spicy food, remove the seeds, then chop finely and put with the garlic.

Wash the pepper and cabbage and drain. Remove the stalk and thick rib of the cabbage then thinly slice both cabbage and pepper. Wipe the mushrooms and cut into quarters.

Put a wok or a heavy pan on a high light and add a tablespoon of olive oil. Add the onion and stir fry or sauté for 2 minutes. Add the garlic, chilli pepper, herbs and spices and cook on for a further 2 minutes.

Add the green pepper and mushrooms and let them cook until tender. If you are not using a wok, turn down the light to avoid burning the mixture.

Open the tin of tomatoes and chop the contents roughly, or use a tin of pre-chopped tomatoes, and add to the pan with the passata and red wine or grape juice. Stir well, then add the cabbage and season to taste. The sauce does not need to cook any further, it will finish off in the oven.

Put the pasta in a large oven or casserole dish and stir in the sauce mixture. Top with grated cheese and put it in the hot oven to cook for 25 to 30 minutes.

Over the last few years this has become one of our most popular pasta dishes, perhaps because it is just that bit different. You can make it vegan by using a vegan cheese or just missing the cheese out. It goes really well with a fresh green salad, and, with a glass of something chilled, makes for a very civilised experience.

# risotto with satay sauce

Now here is a dish that has had more names than you could shake a stick at. It always used to be called a Pilaf and could usually be found tasting of cardamoms and mild curry spices. We also made a version with tomato paste and bay leaves instead of the turmeric and spices. We called this risotto and it was usually served with a Mediterranean style sauce. Over the years the edges seem to have blurred and the two have become one. It is made mainly like the old eastern version but labelled with the Italian name. That's the Eighth Day for you, a land of deep weirdness. If you want to be more traditional in your approach try adding a couple of cardamon pods and a teaspoon of garam masala or Curry powder to the rice with the bay leaves, or miss out the turmeric and add a dessertspoon of tomato purée. You can also ring the changes by serving this with the tomato and coriander sauce from the filo pie recipe. Serves 4 - 6.

8-10oz (225-300g) short grain rice, brown or white
1 large onion
4 oz (100g) mushrooms
1 red pepper
2 courgettes
1 head of broccoli or half a small cauliflower
1 large carrot
2 oz (50g) pumpkin seeds
½ spring cabbage
1 tablespoon turmeric
2 bay leaves
salt and pepper
1 pint (600ml) water
olive oil

Wash and drain the rice, put in a suitable sized pan with the bay leaves, turmeric and a pinch of salt. If you are using brown rice, cover with plenty of cold water, bring to the boil and simmer until done. For white rice, cover with 12-15 floz (350-450ml) cold water and bring to the boil. Cover and allow to cook on the lowest heat until all the water is absorbed, at which point the rice should be cooked.

Peel the onion and chop it finely. Wash the vegetables. If the carrot is not organically grown, peel it. Cut the courgettes and mushrooms into slices, the broccoli into florets, the cabbage into fine shreds and the carrot into thick matchsticks. Cut the pepper in half lengthways, break out the pith and seeds and then cut the halves across their width into slices.

Turn on the oven and set to gas mark 4, 180°C, 350°F. Put the pumpkin seeds on an oven tray, drizzle on a little oil and put them in the oven to brown. Keep your eye on them as you carry on with the rest of the recipe - don't let them burn.

If you have a wok, put it on a high heat with a spot of oil and fry the onion very quickly, stirring all the time. After 1 minute add the pepper, broccoli and carrot, stir fry for another 2 minutes, then add the courgette and mushroom. Cook on for a further minute before turning off the heat.

If you do not have a wok, sauté the vegetables in a frying pan with a little oil, or, if you prefer, you can cook the carrot and broccoli in a little boiling water for a couple of minutes but keep them crispy. Once cooked strain and mix all the vegetables in a large bowl.

Add the shredded cabbage and the toasted seeds to the other vegetables and mix all together with the cooked rice. Put the mixture in an oven proof dish and cover with foil. Cook in the pre-heated oven for 20 to 30 minutes.

While the Risotto is cooking, make the sauce.

# satay sauce

*This easy satay sauce can be used on a variety of dishes. Grilled marinated tofu and a few noodles for example, would be an excellent starter. We would not recommend it with the pea pie, the results could be fatal.*

1 jar (9oz, 250g) of smooth peanut butter
½ large onion, or one small one
1 clove garlic
1 lemon
1 large sprig parsley
¼ pint (150ml) water
2 tablespoons soya sauce
sunflower oil
black pepper
cayenne pepper

Peel and finely chop the onion. Crush or finely chop the garlic. Wash and chop the parsley and squeeze the lemon.

Put a heavy bottomed pan on a medium light, add a dash of oil and fry the onion and garlic until soft.

Add the water, soya sauce, peanut butter and a good pinch of both black and cayenne peppers. Stir the mixture together and bring to the boil.

Simmer for 10 minutes then add the lemon juice and chopped parsley. Cook for a further minute then remove from the heat. If you prefer a really smooth sauce you can blend it before serving.

# mushroom & pepper pizza

Every whole food Café in the world has a variation of that good old vegetarian standby the Pizza. Ours tries to bridge the gap between biscuit-like bases that are sharp enough to sever the tongue of the unwary, and huge wholemeal loaves with the thinnest smear of tomato paste on top. Yes, we've all eaten in those places, they usually have a Lasagne which is about seventy percent brown lentils and as tasty as a door stop. This pizza should end up with enough bread base to make you think you have actually had a meal, and a goodly dollop of really tasty sauce for the enjoyment. Whole food doesn't have to be a penance.
Serves 4 - 6.

**Base**
1 tablespoon dried yeast
2 level teaspoons salt
1 lb (450g) plain wholemeal flour
¾ pint (450ml) warm water

**Topping**
4 oz (100g) mushrooms
1 red or green pepper
1 large onion
1 clove garlic
4 tablespoons tomato purée
2 tomatoes
8 oz (225g) cheddar or mozzarella cheese
1 teaspoon oregano
2 teaspoons basil
salt and pepper
olive oil

Mix flour, salt and dried yeast thoroughly in a bowl. Add half the water and, using your fingers work the mixture up into a dough, adding more water as necessary. Cover the bowl with a tea-towel and leave to rise in a warm place for 30 minutes.

Whilst the dough is rising, make the sauce.
Peel and finely chop the onion and garlic and gently sauté in olive oil with the herbs, until the onion is soft.

Wash and roughly chop the tomatoes and add them to the onions along with the tomato purée. Cover and allow to cook gently for 15 to 20 minutes. Season to taste.

Turn on the oven and let it pre-heat to gas mark 9, 250°C, 500°F.

Wash and slice the mushrooms and pepper. Grate or crumble the cheese.

By now the dough should have risen to twice its original size. Take it out of the bowl and put it on a floured board or work top and knead it thoroughly, using your fists. Work out all the aggression that has built up from reading stupid cookery books and really knock it back. Now roll out onto an oiled baking sheet, either as two pizza shapes or one huge tray full. If rolled thinly this amount of dough will fill the biggest baking sheet your oven can handle. If you have time you can leave the pizza base to stand in the warm for a second rise - another 10 minutes will do - but you can cook it straight away if you are starving.

Spread the sauce mixture on the base and cover with half the cheese. Layer the sliced mushroom and pepper and then top with the rest of the cheese. You can sprinkle on a little olive oil and more oregano if you like.

Bake in the oven for 15 to 20 minutes until the dough has risen and browned.

If you like a richer sauce, finely chop another 4oz (100g) of mushrooms and sauté them with the onions and tomato mixture. The juice will run from the mushroom and add its own delicious flavour to the sauce. This is the traditional Eighth Day method that has stood us in good stead, person and beast, for over twenty five years (Little bit of political correctness there, hope you appreciate it).

# mediterranean potato & spinach bake

*Looking through these recipes it becomes apparent where we go on holiday. Here is another recipe inspired by memories of hot sun, blue sky, stunningly white buildings and, more obviously, the scent of basil and oregano. This dish has all the qualities we search for - it looks good, tastes better and is so simple we can make it! Serves 4 - 6.*

- 2 lb (900g) new potatoes
- 1 large onion
- 2 cloves garlic
- 8 oz (225g) carrots
- 3 sticks celery
- 5 oz (150g) fresh spinach
- 1 tin (14oz, 400g) tomatoes
- 6 oz (175g) grated cheese
- 1 dessertspoon basil
- 1 dessertspoon oregano
- 1 tablespoon red wine vinegar
- 1 tablespoon red grape juice
- 2 tablespoons tomato purée
- olive oil
- salt and pepper

Pre-heat the oven to gas mark 4, 180°C, 350°F.

Scrub the potatoes, put them into a large pan of boiling water and cook until they are just done. Do not over cook. Drain and keep to one side.

Peel the onions and garlic and chop coarsely. Put a heavy bottomed pan on a medium heat, add a tablespoon of olive oil and sauté the onion and garlic until golden.

Wash the carrot, peel if not organic and grate. Wash the celery and chop. Add to the onion and garlic mixture with the herbs and leave to cook for a few minutes.

Add the tinned tomatoes, purée, wine vinegar and grape juice. Bring back to the boil and allow to cook until the celery is soft.

Whilst the sauce is cooking, pull the stalks off the spinach and wash thoroughly. Drain and shred.

Once the sauce is cooked remove from the heat, season to taste and blend into a smooth mixture.

Mix the potato and the spinach in an oven dish. Pour the sauce on top, add the grated cheese and cook in the pre-heated oven for 25 minutes.

At the risk of being boring we will tell you that you can miss out or substitute the cheese to make this a vegan dish. You can use frozen spinach out of season but it really tastes better with fresh. Spinach and potato are one of those great pairings, the Humphrey Bogart and Lauren Bacall of the vegetable world. If you are really indolent you can just mix the cooked potato, spinach, onion and garlic and dress with salt, pepper, olive oil and lemon juice in the Greek style. Eaten hot or cold, on its own or as a side dish it is delicious. Talk about value, we could have put that in as a separate recipe and charged another pound!

# vegetable quiche

*In the old days, we used to call the following dish a flan, now we have to call them quiches or they don't sell. Such is the wonder of European travel, or is it marketing? After all, we were making flans before most Britons had ever heard of Lorraine, let alone its boring quiche. (Little bit of xenophobia there, hope you liked it.) After that pathetic attempt to introduce a long word beginning with x into the publication, we better press on with...*
*Serves 4 - 6.*

**Pastry**
6   oz (150g) self-raising wholemeal flour
3   oz (75g) margarine
3   tablespoons water
    pinch of salt

**Filling**
1   small head broccoli
4   oz (100g) mushrooms
1   red pepper
½   onion
1   teaspoon marjoram or oregano
1   teaspoon basil
4   eggs
½   pint (300ml) milk
8   oz (225g) cheese
    salt and pepper
    olive oil

Mix flour and salt in a suitable bowl. Cut the margarine into small pieces and rub into flour with finger-tips, until it takes on the texture of bread crumbs. Add the water a little at a time and mix into a pliable but not sticky dough. Let it stand for 30 minutes in the fridge before using, if you have the time.

Pre-heat the oven to gas mark 4, 180°C, 350°F.

On a floured surface, roll out the pastry thinly and line an 8 inch flan dish, or ring with it. Make sure you press the pastry firmly into the shape of the tin. Prick the base with a fork and bake for 10 minutes.

Meanwhile, make the filling.

Peel and slice the onion and sauté gently in a little olive oil.

Wash and slice the mushrooms. Wash and cut the broccoli into small florets. When the onions begin to soften, add the mushroom and broccoli and continue to cook for 10 minutes.

Break the eggs into a bowl. Beat well then add the milk and the herbs and beat together.

Put the vegetable filling in the flan dish and add the egg mixture. Cover with cheese and bake for 30 to 40 minutes until the filling has set and the top turned a nice golden brown.

You can, of course eat the Flan hot or cold. It is equally delicious either way. The basic mixture can be varied to suit whatever vegetables you have to hand, within reason of course. Turnip would probably be an acquired taste. Spinach is a favourite, and you can use broccoli, pepper and mushroom on their own. So for a party you could create four separate flans out of the one basic recipe without any problem.

# spaghetti bake

*This is probably the most maligned recipe in this collection. It has been on the menu in the Café since the day we opened and is still a favourite among customers who like the traditional solid Eighth Day whole food style. In the days before menu planning, one legendary worker decided to cook only Spag. Bog, as it was known. He worked - and cooked - nearly every Saturday. This meant that those poor customers who visited every Saturday had virtually a fixed menu. Yet they still came back! Those were the days, consumer choice, what's that? Serves 4 - 6.*

12 oz (350g) spaghetti
1 onion
4 oz (100g) mushrooms
1 carrot
4 oz (100g) dry brown lentils or 8oz (225g) tin
3 cloves garlic
1 level teaspoon oregano
1 level teaspoon basil
1 tin (14oz, 400g) plum tomatoes
1 dessertspoon tomato purée
¼ pint (150ml) tomato juice
oil for frying
salt and pepper
4 oz (100g) grated cheese

Soak the lentils overnight, if you can and then cook until tender but not mushy. They will cook un-soaked but take a lot longer. If using tinned lentils, drain first and rinse.

Put a large pan of salted water on to heat and bring to the boil. Break the dry spaghetti into short pieces and add to the pan. Stir well to stop the pasta clumping together, then partially cover and cook, using just less than the recommended time on the packet. It needs to be only just cooked, definitely not overdone. Once cooked, drain and then put it back in the pan and stir in a teaspoon or so of olive oil, to keep it separate. Put the lid on the pan and leave until you need it.

Whilst the spaghetti is cooking, you can start on the sauce.
Peel and chop the onion finely. Peel and crush the garlic and fry together until the onion becomes clear.

Wash or wipe the mushrooms and chop or slice. Add to the onions with the herbs and fry on for a couple of minutes.

Liquidise or chop up the tomatoes and add to the pan along with the purée and tomato juice. Allow the mixture to simmer for 10 minutes.

Wash and peel the carrot if not organic, then grate and add it to the sauce. Now mix in the cooked lentils and season the mixture to taste. The sauce should be tasty but a sloppy, thin consistency - add more tomato juice if necessary.

Next put the cooked spaghetti in an oven dish and pour on the sauce. Stir it to mix in the pasta. Cover with the grated cheese and bake for 20 to 25 minutes at gas mark 4, 180°C, 350°F until the cheese has melted and the top has browned.

The only point to watch out for, to create the perfect spag. bog, is to keep the sauce runny. It will all be absorbed or evaporate as it cooks. So if you have too little liquid in at the start, you will end up with a cake at the end - tasty but solid.

# nut roast

*In the introduction to this section we mentioned a legendary member who cooked a different bake every time, so it is only fitting that we should end with his finest creation - nut roast. As is usual with our recipes, he made it first at home and used up all the bits of vegetables he had left over. The results were so good that he developed it at work, with a bit of trial and error, until he settled on the combination of nuts and vegetables that gave the best taste. This is the basic recipe we use today. When you are making a hundred portions per batch, one aubergine more or less does not matter. To reduce it back to a domestic level is more difficult. If you cannot use exactly the same quantity of vegetables, do not panic, it will work with different combinations, so long as the total weight is the same. It is still a good recipe for using up left-overs. Any cooked vegetables you have can be included in the total bulk. If you want to use more expensive nuts, feel free - we use peanuts as the bulk because they are more economical. For a special occasion you can go mad and use whatever nuts you want. Serves 4 - 6.*

- 1 lb (450g) peanuts
- 8 oz (225g) hazelnuts or walnuts
- 8 oz (225g) red lentils
- 2 oz (50g) aubergine
- 2 sticks celery
- 1 medium carrot
- 1 medium courgette
- 1 small onion
- 2 cloves garlic
- 4 oz (100g) mushroom
- bunch of parsley
- 4 oz (100g) breadcrumbs
- 2 teaspoon oregano
- 1 teaspoon thyme
- 1 teaspoon marjoram
- 1 teaspoon paprika
- 2 tablespoon soy sauce
- 2 tablespoon sunflower oil
- salt and pepper

First of all wash and drain the lentils. Cover with cold water, bring to the boil and simmer until cooked.

Grate or chop the nuts and keep to one side.

Wash all the vegetables, peeling if necessary. Grate the carrot and celery and finely chop everything else.

Fry the onions and garlic in a heavy pan until soft. Add the mushrooms, chopped herbs, spices, seasoning and aubergine. Cook gently until the aubergine is soft. If your pan is big enough, add the rest of the vegetables and cook on for 10 minutes - if not put the cooked vegetables in a mixing bowl and sauté those remaining for 10 minutes, then mix together at the end.

Stir in the soy sauce and add the nuts and breadcrumbs. Mix all together evenly. The mixture should be wet but not sloppy. If it is too dry moisten with a little vegetable stock or water.

Put into an oiled loaf tin and cover with foil. Bake for 45 minutes at gas mark 5, 190°C, 375°F.

Serve with either mushroom gravy (page 45), Tomato and Coriander sauce (page 50) or with either of the two sauces given below.

# sweet pepper sauce

2 large red peppers
1 small onion
3 cloves garlic
1 tin (14oz, 400g) tomatoes
sunflower oil
salt and pepper

Peel and chop the onion and garlic and fry gently in a little oil.

Wash, de-seed and chop the pepper and add to the onions Cook for 10 minutes then add the tomatoes and a pinch of salt and pepper.

Allow to cook for a further 5 to 10 minutes, then blend and adjust the seasoning.

If you like a more tangy sauce, include half a chilli pepper with the red pepper or add a pinch of chilli powder.

# onion gravy

1 large onion
1 oz (25g) margarine
1 heaped tablespoon flour
10 floz (300ml) water or vegetable stock
1 bay leaf
pinch dried sage
salt and pepper
dash of shoyu

Peel and chop the onion. Melt the margarine in a heavy pan and sauté the onion with the sage and bay leaf for 5 minutes.

Stir in the flour and cook for another 10 minutes until the onion is very soft and the flour has browned. Keep your eye on it and stir when necessary. Do not let the flour burn.

Now gradually add the water, stirring to prevent lumps, and bring to the boil. Add the shoyu and seasoning and cook for another 10 minutes. Remove the bay leaf and serve as it is or blend into a smooth sauce.

With these different sauces, you can adapt the one roast to a variety of menus. Serve with plain boiled rice and a pepper sauce, for example, or go for the full monty, with roast potatoes, Yorkshire pudding and gravy. Either way it is a rich and delicious meal - a fitting finale to our bake section.

# puddings

*The words "sweet" and "dessert" do not really suit our Café style of cookery. They will always be puddings of the old school but made without the old school's suet. As a health conscious group, we do not recommend sweet things in general and too many are obviously bad for you. But it is nice to indulge yourself in a sticky pudding every once in a while. As our contribution to the great sugar debate, we always sweeten our puddings with muscovado or one of the other less processed sugars. We feel that at least they do contain some minerals as well as empty calories. We keep them mostly vegan and so do not use honey. You can substitute honey, corn syrup or malt for the sugar. You will have to experiment a little to find the proportion and taste you like.*

*Puddings are like pies - the British contribution to the world's pool of good things to eat. They seem to have their origins in the savoury and highly spiced concoctions of our medieval and Tudor ancestors. These meat and fruit porridges were, over the course of time, transmogrified into the sweet and meatless puds of the Victorian age - via Mrs. Beeton to Eighth Day.*

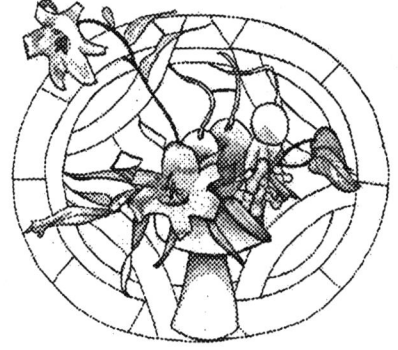

# sponge puddings

*The first three puddings are all variations on a theme of sponge. Not a real sponge, but an easy to make, vegan sponge which we adopted years ago and have made ever since. It rises a treat and never gives any problems, despite not having any eggs in it. Non-vegans can substitute honey for the sugar or you can use concentrated apple juice, but it does tend to interfere with the rise - which is why we have stuck with sugar. Serves 4 - 6.*

### Basic sponge mixture
- 4 oz (100g) white self-raising flour
- 4 oz (100g) wholemeal self-raising flour
- 4 oz (100g) margarine
- 4 oz (100g) muscovado or soft brown sugar
- 2 oz (50g) dried fruit - currants, raisins, sultanas
- 1 teaspoon baking powder
- 1 teaspoon ground ginger
- 4 to 6 floz (125-175ml) cold water or apple juice

Mix together the dry ingredients, including the dried fruit, in a mixing bowl, until everything is evenly distributed.

Melt the margarine and add to the dry mix. Then add the water until a runny cake mixture consistency is reached.

Now proceed to any of the following varieties:

## pear & ginger sponge

1 lb (450g) Pears

Wash and thinly slice the pears and layer on the bottom of a greased, oven-proof bowl.

Pour the sponge mixture over the pears, cover with foil and cook for 25 minutes on gas mark 4, 180°C, 350°F. Cut round the top with a knife and turn out onto a plate to serve.

# apple sponge

Use the basic mix but add 1 teaspoon ground cinnamon to the dry ingredients. Then take 1 lb (450g) baking apples.

Method as pear sponge.

# spicy fruit pudding

Use the basic mixture but add 1 teaspoon mixed spice, and 4oz more dried fruit to the dry mix. Carry on as before and then pour the mixture into a greased, oven-proof bowl and bake as for the pear sponge.

You can ring the changes with these puddings, to suit the fruit you have to hand. Blueberry for example, makes an excellent pudding, just miss out the dried fruit and add 6oz (150g) fresh or frozen blueberries.

# apple crumble

*A logical follow on from sponge would be rubber, but instead we change the texture to crumble. It is one of those deeply philosophical problems - a bit like the chicken and the egg (for vegans the soya bean and the tofu). Which came first, the pie or the crumble? Did someone forget to put the water in the pastry for an apple pie, or did they spill water into the crumble? These questions trouble philosopher cooks in the still watches of the night. Serves 4 - 6.*

- 8 oz (225g) flour - plain wholemeal
- 4 oz (100g) margarine
- 2 oz (50g) muscovado or soft brown sugar
- 1 lb (450g) baking apples

Wash, core and chop the apples into chunks. Put in a pan with 4 tablespoons of water and a little lemon juice. Put on moderate heat and leave to stew for 5 minutes or so, stirring occasionally. The apple should be just starting to soften, not becoming a pulp.

Mix the flour and margarine with the fingertips until it is like the texture of breadcrumbs. Add the sugar and mix.

Put the cooked apples in a greased pie dish and sprinkle with a little more sugar. Cover with the crumble mixture.

Bake in the oven at gas mark 5, 190°C, 375°F for 30 to 40 minutes, or until brown on top.

This recipe can be used to make any sort of fruit crumble. For example rhubarb - just substitute the apples with 1 lb of washed and chopped rhubarb for every 4 people and treat it in exactly the same way. Other varieties could include blackcurrant, blueberry, blackberry and apple, almost anything you like really.

# apple pie

*Here is the other half of the equation, an apple pie. This one is traditional in having a top and bottom crust. You can make half the pastry, and only put on a top crust, if you wish. Whatever you do, it will be delicious. Serves 4.*

**Pastry**
8 oz (225g) wholemeal self-raising flour
4 oz (100g) margarine
4 tablespoons water
pinch salt

3 large baking apples
2 tablespoons brown sugar
$1/2$ teaspoon ground cloves

Put the flour into a mixing bowl and add salt (optional). Cut the margarine into small pieces and rub into the flour with your finger-tips, until it resembles breadcrumbs. Add the water, a little at a time and form into a dough. Do not make it too sticky. It is better if you can let it stand for half an hour in the fridge before using.

While the pastry sits in the fridge, wash core and slice the apples. If you like your pie filling firm, leave them alone. If you like a soft filling, cook them in 1 tablespoon of water for 5 to 10 minutes.

Lightly grease or oil an 8 inch pie dish. Take half the pastry and roll out thinly on a floured surface, line the bottom of the dish. Cut off the excess and keep to one side.

Put the apples on the bottom crust and sprinkle with sugar and cloves. Turn on the oven to preheat to gas mark 5, 190ºC, 375ºF.

Roll out the rest of the pastry and cover the apples. Trim round and pinch the edges together. Use the trimmings to make leaf shapes (or the silhouette of your favourite film star) to decorate the top. Brush with oil if you want a golden pastry top. Finally cut a small slit in the top to allow the steam to escape. Bake for about 30 minutes until golden brown.

Once again you can make up any fruit filling you like, blackberry and apple is the autumnal favourite, and what about gooseberry? Nothing better, especially with a nice drop of custard.

# tofu lemon cheesecake

*Over the last decade or more, we have had phases of making cheesecakes. They come and go without much reference to the changing seasons or the sun spot cycle or anything else really. What seems to happen is that a Café worker gets fired with enthusiasm and makes a cheesecake - we all think it is brilliant and say how much we all missed it. No-one can understand why it is not made regularly and the Café decide to make cheesecake every day from now on. A week later everybody is fed up with trying to fit cheesecake-making into the routine, and it disappears without trace, until the next time. Still, it means that when we do make them, they have the advantage of novelty! We always produce vegan cheesecakes so all our customers can eat them and have tried many different recipes. This one is a fairly recent arrival but has the great advantage of giving consistently delicious results. Serves 4.*

**Base**
12 oz (350g) digestive biscuits
6 oz (175g) melted margarine

**Filling**
1 packet plain tofu
   juice and rind of 2 lemons
2 oz (50g) cornflour
3 tablespoons golden syrup
3/4 pint (450ml) water

To make the base, crumble the biscuits into a bowl, melt the margarine and add to the biscuit crumbs. Mix and press into a well-greased, 8 inch diameter flan tin. Try not to get a thick welt where the sides meet the base. Set on one side to cool.

Put the water, golden syrup and cornflour in a pan. Heat gradually to boiling point, stirring well to avoid lumps. When boiling, reduce the heat and allow to thicken.

Once the mixture has thickened, add the tofu and lemon and blend until creamy. Pour into the base and chill.

This cheesecake is good as it is, but for a really special treat, top with black currants, raspberries or similar fresh fruit.

# apple strudel

*Here is another recipe that we do not make often enough in the Café. We first started making strudel years ago and, after some experimental versions, settled on this one - which is fairly authentic. When we first made it, we also made authentic strudel dough using olive oil and flour. Which, although very pleasant to eat, is a bit of a bind to make in a busy kitchen. So we went on to filo which is a lot easier to manage. Serves 6.*

- 1 lb (450g) baking apples
- 3 tablespoons currants
- 1 tablespoon breadcrumbs
- 1 dessertspoon muscovado sugar
- juice from half a lemon
- 2 oz (50g) margarine
- 1 dessertspoon chopped almonds
- 4 sheets filo pastry

Thaw out the filo pastry. Keep cold and covered with a damp cloth or cling film. Wash, core and cut the apples into very thin slices.

Take a little of the margarine and melt in a pan. Brown the breadcrumbs and mix with the apples, currants, almonds and sugar. Moisten with the lemon juice.

Melt the rest of the margarine.

Lay the first sheet of filo pastry on a clean tea towel and brush with melted margarine. Lay on the next sheet and brush and so on until the end. Cover the pastry with the apple mixture. Lift the corner of the cloth, ease your fingers under the sheets of filo and roll the whole rectangle into a crescent shape. Slide the strudel off the tea towel and onto an oiled baking sheet. Brush the top with the remainder of the melted margarine and bake for 20 minutes at gas mark 7, 220°C, 425°F then reduce oven to gas mark 4, 180°C 350°F, and bake for a further 20 minutes.

This is delicious served hot or cold and will keep for several days in an air tight container.

# superior victorian christmas pudding

*This pudding will re-appear if we ever get around to doing a Christmas recipe book, but we thought we would put it in as it is such a brilliant recipe. We make it once a year, in trays, for our Café Christmas dinner menu - scaled up enormously of course. Like a lot of our previous recipes this started in the home of one of our cooks. Working from a Mrs. Beeton original, which had about half a ton of suet as its main ingredient, it was refined into this wonderful, very rich, but vegetarian version, more suited to our modern palate. The original family sized recipe has been in use as the finishing touch to Christmas dinner every year for at least 20 years, and still tastes every bit as sensational as the first time. Serves 6.*

10 oz (300g) breadcrumbs-
   (1 small loaf with the crusts cut off)
8 oz (225g) muscovado sugar
12 oz (350g) dried fruit
4 oz (100g) margarine
1 level teaspoon mixed spice
1 level teaspoon ground cinnamon
good pinch of nutmeg-
   (2 grates of a fresh nutmeg!)
2 level dessertspoons molasses
2 eggs (or 4 tablespoons sunflower
   oil for a vegan pudding)
juice from half a lemon
1 teaspoon of lime juice (optional)
$1/2$ wine glass rum or brandy or
   10 drops rum essence

Mix all the dry ingredients together in a good size mixing bowl. Add the eggs and all the liquids. Stir the mixture well until thoroughly mixed and of an even colour. Don't forget to make a wish as you stir it! Once mixed and wished over, put it in a pudding basin, cover with greaseproof paper or foil and bake for 2 hours at gas mark 1, 140°C, 275°F.

If you can arrange to put the pudding basin into a larger oven proof container, with enough water to fill up the space between the two, and cover the whole thing with another layer of kitchen foil, the results will be even better, as you will have kept the moisture in the pudding.

Rich puddings like this store very well if kept sealed in a cool place, or frozen and so were always made well in advance of Christmas and reheated. To reheat first allow to thaw naturally if frozen and then put the pudding, in its bowl, in a large pan of water. Cover and steam for $3/4$ to 1 hour. If possible stand the pudding basin on something heat proof, to keep it off the bottom of the pan - a jam jar lid will do. This will keep the heat spread evenly.

# cumberland rum butter

*The following recipe has nothing to do with Eighth Day at all, but is a traditional hard sauce for a traditional pudding so we make no apologies for including it. Rum butter is the sort of thing you can make in advance. You can even give it as a gift, to such of your relations as would appreciate the ardent spirits, as Mrs. Beeton might have said.*

4 oz (100g) butter
½ teaspoon grated nutmeg
6 oz (150g) caster sugar
¼ teaspoon ground cinnamon
½ wine glass rum

Mix the spices with the caster sugar. Warm the butter until it can just be poured, but not actually hot. Pour it onto the caster sugar, beating thoroughly until it is smooth. Add the glass of rum and beat well again. Pour into ramekins or other suitable containers. When set dredge with caster sugar. This will keep for a month in the refrigerator. You can substitute vegan margarine for the butter. This will not need warming and should just be beaten with the sugar and spice. It will stay softer than the butter version.

A big blob of rum butter on the hot Christmas pudding, a slurp of cream, Christmas bliss!

Similar hard sauces can be made with butter or margarine and fruit for eating with the baked puddings given earlier. A typical version would be to use:

4oz (100 g) butter
6oz (150 g) caster sugar
4oz (100 g) blueberries

Beat all together until it becomes a smooth purple paste, then allow to set for a few minutes before eating. Delicious for a really unhealthy treat.

# Index

| | |
|---|---|
| Apple, beetroot salad and | 35 |
| Apple crumble | 73 |
| Apple pie | 74 |
| Apple sponge | 72 |
| Apple Strudel | 76 |
| Aubergine, chickpea curry and | 25 |
| | |
| Basil, tomato soup and | 14 |
| Béchamel sauce | 47 |
| Beetroot and apple salad | 35 |
| Broccoli and orange salad | 37 |
| Broccoli soup | 12 |
| Butter bean bake | 48 |
| | |
| Carribean stew | 19 |
| Carrot and coriander soup | 10 |
| Cauliflower and lentil bake | 43 |
| Chickpea and aubergine curry | 25 |
| Chickpea peasant salad | 38 |
| Christmas pudding | 77 |
| Coconut, lentil soup and | 13 |
| Coriander, carrot soup and | 10 |
| Coriander and tomato sauce with filo pie | 50 |
| Cumberland rum butter | 78 |
| | |
| Filo pie with coriander and tomato sauce | 50 |
| French dressing | 36 |
| French onion soup | 16 |

| | |
|---|---|
| Gravy, onion | 69 |
| | |
| Hungarian goulash | 21 |
| | |
| Kidney beans, spicy salad | 33 |
| Kimpira stew, Japanese | 27 |
| | |
| Lemon tofu cheesecake | 75 |
| Lentil, cauliflower bake and | 43 |
| Lentil and coconut soup | 13 |
| | |
| Mediterranean stew | 29 |
| Mediterranean rice salad | 40 |
| Mediterranean potato and spinach bake | 60 |
| Mint, split pea soup and | 11 |
| Mulligatawny | 15 |
| Mushroom and pepper pizza | 58 |
| Mushroom gravy, with pea pie | 45 |
| | |
| Nut roast | 66 |
| | |
| Onion soup, French | 16 |
| Onion gravy | 69 |
| On The Eighth Day salad dressing | 41 |
| Orange, broccoli salad and | 37 |
| | |
| Pasta salad, Italian | 39 |
| Pasta arrabiata | 53 |
| Pea Pie with mushroom gravy | 45 |
| Persian pea soup | 11 |
| Pizza, mushroom and pepper | 58 |
| Potato and spinach Mediterranean bake | 60 |
| Pudding, Christmas | 77 |
| Pudding, spicy fruit | 72 |

| | |
|---|---|
| Quiche vegetable | 62 |
| | |
| Raita | 25 |
| Rice á la Quay Co-op salad | 34 |
| Rice salad, Mediterranean | 40 |
| Risotto with satay sauce | 55 |
| Rum butter, Cumberland | 78 |
| | |
| Salad dressing On The Eighth Day | 41 |
| Satay sauce with risotto | 55 |
| Spaghetti bake | 64 |
| Spicy fruit pudding | 72 |
| Spinach and potato Mediterranean bake | 60 |
| Split pea and mint soup | 11 |
| Sponge, pear & ginger | 71 |
| Sponge, apple | 72 |
| Sweet pepper sauce | 68 |
| | |
| Tofu lemon cheesecake | 75 |
| Tofu Mattar Paneer | 23 |
| Tomato and basil soup | 14 |
| | |
| Vegetable quiche | 62 |
| Victorian christmas pudding | 77 |